Jane Butcher was born in Denver, USA, but grew up and was educated in the UK, spending most of her childhood actively involved in sport. She trained as a secondary school teacher and taught PE and RE in a city secondary school. Having also trained as a youth worker, she moved into full-time church-based children's and youth work in 1993. Over the next ten years, her posts included Children's Worker at a church in Michigan, USA, and six years as the Children's Worker at St John's Church, Harborne, Birmingham. Jane joined the Barnabas children's ministry team in September 2007. In her spare time she enjoys cooking and making the most of the wide variety of restaurants in Birmingham.

Messy Church is growing! Every month, families who have never set foot in a church before are enjoying Messy Church, and every month more Messy Churches are started all over the UK and worldwide. Messy Church is proving effective in sharing God's good news with families across denominations and church traditions. We estimate that some 100,000 people belong to Messy Churches—and the number is growing all the time. For more information about Messy Church, visit www.messychurch.org.uk.

Messy Church is enabled, resourced and supported by BRF (Bible Reading Fellowship), a Registered Charity, as one of its core ministries. BRF makes Messy Church freely available and derives no direct income from the work that we do to support it in the UK and abroad.

Would you be willing to support this ministry with your prayer and your giving? To find out more, please visit www.messychurch.org.uk/champions.

Messy Church® is a registered word mark and the logo is a registered device mark of The Bible Reading Fellowship.

Text copyright © Jane Butcher 2011
The author asserts the moral right
to be identified as the author of this work

Published by
The Bible Reading Fellowship
15 The Chambers, Vineyard
Abingdon OX14 3FE
United Kingdom
Tel: +44 (0)1865 319700
Email: enquiries@brf.org.uk
Website: www.brf.org.uk
BRF is a Registered Charity

ISBN 978 0 85746 069 1

First published 2011
This edition 2011
10 9 8 7 6 5 4 3 2 1 0
All rights reserved

A catalogue record for this book is available from the British Library

Printed in Singapore by Craft Print International Ltd

The paper used in the production of this publication was supplied by mills that source their raw materials from sustainably managed forests. Soy-based inks were used in its printing and the laminate film is biodegradable.

Messy Cooks

A handbook
for Messy Church catering teams

Jane Butcher

For Katie, who makes home cooking so rewarding

Acknowledgments

With grateful thanks to all who have contributed to this book—in particular, Lucy Moore; Charis Lambert and Janet Lane from Morden Messy Church; Chris Rees and team from Dronfield Messy Church.

And a thank you to Messy Church catering teams…

Oh no… what will we have for tea? At the end of a busy day of working, rushing around at home, running children from one activity to the next, this is often the last thing on people's minds. To come to Messy Church and not to have to think about that question will be such a relief! The role of the Messy Church catering team is so valuable in many ways—not only practically but also in what it says about welcome and hospitality. We hope that these recipes and ideas that have been tested in a Messy Church setting will encourage and resource you and your teams. Many of the recipes that have come from the Morden Messy Church have been served to 150 people at a time. You may be catering for fewer but the recipes can be adjusted accordingly, and the ever-valuable tips on how to increase amounts when suddenly faced with more people than expected will be at your fingertips. It only remains for us to say 'thank you' for all you do with Messy Church.

Messy quotes

'The girls love Messy Church and can't wait until the next one.'

Broomfield Messy Church, Chelmsford

'One of the things we have recently introduced is to ask our older church members, who cannot physically get involved with Messy Church, to pray for us on the day of our Messy Church. Last time we gave out prayer cards and we believe that this has made such a difference. It makes our elderly members feel a part of Messy Church and we have certainly felt the Holy Spirit moving and the atmosphere change at Messy Church since this has been happening. It is great to think that everyone, in the mayhem that is Messy Church, is being held up before God in prayer.'

Broomfield Messy Church, Chelmsford

'At St Andrew's Messy Church we have been following the story of Joseph and his brothers, and decided that the next time we met we would attempt to make a model of a pyramid, if we could find a suitable template. Two weeks later, in the local supermarket, Joel, aged eight, came running up the aisle shouting, "I know how to make a pyramid!" For our final look at Joseph, we decided to incorporate junk modelling; once again, Joel was first with his suggestion to make Pharaoh's Palace.'

Andover Methodist Circuit Messy Church

'Our Messy Church is often complete pandemonium! Still, God shows up and draws people closer to him.'

Judy Paulsen, Christ Church, Oshawa, Ontario, Canada

'I have a fond childhood memory of my mum making Yorkshire puddings and always having enough batter over to make some delicious Yorkshire puddings with currants and jam for dessert—you'll find the recipe on page 72.'

Janet Lane, Messy Church, Morden Baptist Church

Contents

Messy mains

Messy desserts

Foreword

Food and Christian mission: it's always been a great combination, ever since the day when Levi the apostle threw an impromptu banquet so that his tax collector friends could meet with Jesus (Luke 5:29). At the heart of Christian worship is the Eucharist, a call to renewed faith, love and obedience combined with bread broken and wine outpoured; and, from the days of the early church to the present day, the combination of sharing a meal and sharing Jesus as the Bread of Life has proved a grace and blessing to believers and seekers alike.

Of course, things could get a little out of hand in the early church. Jesus had to remind his contemporaries to be inclusive in their guest lists, and not to head for the top table at the meals they attended (Luke 14:13; Matthew 23:6). Paul had to challenge the greedier members of the church in Corinth not to scoff their meals but to leave enough for everybody else (1 Corinthians 11:21). But when it worked well, it worked very well—and it's no coincidence that the church where the Christians 'broke bread in their homes and ate together with glad and sincere hearts' was the same church of which we read, 'The Lord added to their number daily those who were being saved' (Acts 2:46–47).

As someone for whom food and Christian mission are 'two of my favourite things', I am delighted to commend Jane Butcher's book. So much teaching about Christian mission is educational, thoughtful, even inspiring, without ever answering the question, 'Yes, but how?', so any resources that answer the 'how' questions are to be warmly welcomed. Messy Church has been practical from its inception, as well as embracing the great Christian principles of all-age mission and hands-on discipleship. So a loud 'Hallelujah!' for this latest addition to the Messy Church toolkit!

+Andrew Watson, Bishop of Aston

Introduction

Welcome to *Messy Cooks*—the handbook for everyone involved in Messy Church catering teams! We hope you will find that this book is a useful treasure store of practical and easy-to-prepare recipes for all the Messy Church events you are planning.

All the recipes are made with readily available, inexpensive ingredients and do not require hours to prepare or cook. The book also includes recipes suitable for vegetarians and people with special dietary requirements, such as those with wheat or dairy intolerance. Each recipe idea is ethical, in that it doesn't use food wastefully, and is accompanied by suggestions as to how the dish can be adapted to provide further ideas and variations on the theme.

The material also includes helpful information about basic cooking skills, quantities, weights and measures, essential equipment and health and safety, as well as an index for all the recipes, plus space for you to jot down your own personal reflections, comments and notes. Finally, there are some ideas for fun and creative ways to include food activities to illustrate or emphasise a particular theme or Bible story.

The book gives a wealth of recipes for main meals and the all-important desserts, as well as ideas for easy snacks and dessert options. All the recipes will feed a family of four to five people and are designed to appeal to different tastes, occasions and seasons of the year. The recipes can be sized up for your Messy Church events, but families can also enjoy them at home by using the basic quantities suggested.

Why Messy meals?

You may wonder whether providing food at Messy Church is really essential. Well, apart from the positive feedback (no pun intended) that you might receive, such as 'It's the best bit—eating with my friends' (from a four-year-old), 'It's always yummy' (from a seven-year-old), or 'I don't have to cook when we get home' (from a relieved mum), sharing food together is also biblical. There are many examples in the Bible of stories being told and relationships developed around a meal.

Eating together offers hospitality and welcome; it allows people the chance to engage with others, develop relationships and perhaps discuss all that's been happening at Messy Church. Messy Church meals encourage families to eat together and, on a purely practical level, mean that the leaders don't have to go home and start cooking a meal after a hard session's work.

Furthermore, while there are different situations and limitations in every church, it's worth looking at your food provision once in a while and asking if there are any ways you can use the opportunity better to provide a warm welcome as a witness to Jesus' own hospitality. Yes, there may be disasters—times when the baked potatoes are far from 'baked', you overestimate the quantities and end up having to eat chilli for a week, or your lovely baking becomes more of a pancake than a chocolate cake—but it's what's at the heart of the eating together that matters. Sitting together to eat at a table is a cornerstone of Messy Church. The very act of eating together says so much about being community, being family and being open-handed. It provides a valuable opportunity to begin forming lasting relationships. So often, food unites people, puts them at ease and provides a springboard to conversation.

If you haven't yet felt brave enough to eat together at Messy Church, our hope is that this book will provide a starting point for you to give it a try and see what happens. For those of you who already provide food, we hope that this book will be a helpful addition to new ideas.

Easy snack options

For the days when making up dishes from recipes seems a step too far, here are some easy snack options that might fit the bill.

- Homemade or shop-bought soups
- Sandwiches or baps with a variety of fillings, such as cheese and pickle, tuna and cucumber, ham and mustard, hummus and tomato, or cooked chicken and salad, served with crisps and wedges of apple
- New potatoes, baked beans and sausage rolls
- Baked potatoes with a variety of fillings, such as baked beans, tuna with mayonnaise and sweet corn, ratatouille, coleslaw and so on, served with salad

However you use this book, enjoy the food, enjoy the fellowship and enjoy the fast-moving (and sometimes frantic) fun that makes Messy Church what it is.

Food hygiene

When it comes to food preparation, churches are not exempt from health and safety legislation. It is important that all members of your catering team are given training in food hygiene, health and safety in kitchen areas and first aid. Contact your local authority for advice, guidance and information about training for members of your catering team. Ecclesiastical Insurance Group also offers guidelines for churches about food preparation and general health and safety. They can be contacted as follows:

Ecclesiastical Insurance Group
Beaufort House
Brunswick Road
Gloucester
GL1 1JZ

Telephone: 0845 777 3322
Website: www.ecclesiastical.com

The Food Standards Agency also has information about food hygiene and legislation. Visit their website at www.food.gov.uk.

Conversion tables

The following tables show approximate conversions, rounded up or down. Never mix metric and imperial measures in one recipe: use one system or the other.

All spoon measurements in the recipes are level unless otherwise specified. Abbreviations are as follows:

- Teaspoon: tsp
- Dessertspoon: dsp
- Tablespoon: tbsp

Weight

Imperial	Metric
½ oz	10 g
¾ oz	20 g
1 oz	25 g
1½ oz	40 g
2 oz	50 g
2½ oz	60 g
3 oz	75 g
4 oz	110 g
4½ oz	125 g
5 oz	150 g
6 oz	175 g
7 oz	200 g
8 oz	225 g
9 oz	250 g
10 oz	275 g
12 oz	350 g
1 lb	450 g
1 lb 8 oz	700 g
2 lb	900 g
3 lb	1.35 kg

Volume

Imperial	Metric
2 fl oz	55 ml
3 fl oz	75 ml
5 fl oz (¼ pint)	150 ml
10 fl oz (½ pint)	275 ml
1 pint	570 ml
1¼ pint	725 ml
1¾ pint	1 litre
2 pint	1.2 litre
2½ pint	1.5 litre
4 pint	2.25 litres

Oven temperatures

NB: If using a fan oven, you will need to reduce the oven temperature by 20 degrees.

Gas Mark	°F	°C
1	275°F	140°C
2	300°F	150°C
3	325°F	170°C
4	350°F	180°C
5	375°F	190°C
6	400°F	200°C
7	425°F	220°C
8	450°F	230°C
9	475°F	240°C

Dimensions

Imperial	Metric
⅛ inch	3 mm
¼ inch	5 mm
½ inch	1 cm
¾ inch	2 cm
1 inch	2.5 cm
1¼ inch	3 cm
1½ inch	4 cm
1¾ inch	4.5 cm
2 inch	5 cm
2½ inch	6 cm
3 inch	7.5 cm
3½ inch	9 cm
4 inch	10 cm
5 inch	13 cm
5¼ inch	13.5 cm
6 inch	15 cm
6½ inch	16 cm
7 inch	18 cm
7½ inch	19 cm
8 inch	20 cm
9 inch	23 cm
9½ inch	24 cm
10 inch	25.5 cm
11 inch	28 cm
12 inch	30 cm

Basic cooking skills

Shortcrust pastry

- 250g plain flour
- Pinch of salt
- 125g margarine (or a 50–50 mixture of margarine and lard)
- 4–5 tbsp cold water

Method

1. Using a light touch, rub the fat into the flour until a crumb consistency is formed.
2. Gradually add cold water until the mixture binds together.
3. Gather into a ball, but do not knead the dough.
4. Roll out on a floured surface, using a floured rolling pin.

Variations

- Use a beaten egg to bind the dough instead of water.
- For a sweet dessert pastry, add 50g caster sugar.
- For a chocolate pastry, add 50g caster sugar and 25g cocoa powder.

Gravy

- 1 stock cube
- 275ml water (if you are cooking vegetables, use the water that these have been cooked in)
- 1 rounded tbsp cornflour
- Cold water

Method

1. In a pan, dissolve the stock cube in water.
2. In a separate bowl, blend the cornflour with the cold water until smooth.
3. Gradually add the cornflour mixture to the stock, stirring constantly until blended. Heat gently until thickened.

Variations

- Add a dash of balsamic vinegar for a darker colour and taste.
- Add 1 tsp of mild mustard.
- If you are cooking meat, add the juices once the fat has been strained off.

Economic garlic bread

- Baguettes
- Butter or margarine
- Dried garlic or garlic granules

Method

1. Slice baguettes.
2. Mix butter/margarine with garlic or garlic granules. Spread through the slices and bake for a few minutes until the butter melts and the baguettes are crispy.

Chocolate sauce

- 50g butter or margarine
- 50g cocoa powder
- 50g muscovado sugar
- 1 tbsp squeezy golden syrup
- 150ml milk

Method

1. In a pan, dissolve the cocoa powder in the butter.
2. Add the golden syrup and heat gently.
3. Gradually add the milk and mix to blend. Do not allow to boil.
4. Serve hot or cold.

Variations

- Omit the cocoa powder for a butterscotch alternative.

Basic biscuit dough

- 200g self-raising flour
- 100g caster sugar
- 100g margarine
- 1 egg (beaten)

Optional additions (choose one)

- 1 tsp lemon juice
- 50g currants
- 50g chocolate chips
- 1 tsp grated orange rind

Method

1. Rub the margarine into the flour. Stir in the sugar. Add the egg and optional ingredients as desired. Mix to a stiff dough.
2. Knead the dough lightly and then roll out on a floured surface.
3. Cut out dough using shaped biscuit cutters of your choice.
4. Transfer to oiled greaseproof paper on a baking tray.
5. Bake for 15 minutes at gas mark 4 (180°C / 350°F).

Easy icing for cakes and biscuits

- 100g icing sugar (plus extra as required)
- 1 tbsp cocoa powder (optional)
- Natural food colouring (optional)
- Water

Method

1. Mix icing sugar with a few drops of lukewarm water and stir. Add more icing sugar or water until the consistency is thick. It will thicken slightly more on standing.
2. Stir in a few drops of food colouring or cocoa powder to add colour or flavour.

Basic useful amounts per serving

The following amounts are for adult portions: halve the quantities for a child.

- Pasta: 50g per person
- Couscous: 50g per person
- Long grain rice: 50g per person
- Basmati rice: 75g per person
- Carrots: 1 per person
- Potatoes: 1 per person
- Onions: 1 for up to four people
- Stock cubes: 1 for up to four people

For rice, an alternative measurement is to use half a mug of rice and a full mug of water per adult (that is, double the amount of water to rice). Bring to the boil, cover, turn the heat down to the lowest setting and leave for 10–15 minutes until the water has been absorbed. No need to drain—simply fluff with a fork.

Essential ingredients to have on hand

- Salt and pepper (for seasoning)
- Dried herbs
- Stock cubes
- Cornflour (for thickening gravy and sauces)

Items to have on hand if a greater quantity of food is suddenly required

- Tins of tomatoes are inexpensive, have a long shelf life, and can be added to a variety of recipes, such as chilli, bolognaise or shepherd's pie, to give greater volume.
- Tins of baked beans are also inexpensive, with a long shelf life. Use as above or as an additional vegetable if needed.
- Tins of condensed soup can be quickly added to give extra volume and flavour to a sauce. Use tomato for a vegetarian-based recipe and chicken for a chicken or tuna recipe.
- Couscous only takes five minutes to cook and doesn't require a pan. Simply place in a bowl and add boiling water (though stock gives a nicer flavour). Fluff with a fork and serve as an alternative to rice or pasta.
- Extra bread or bread rolls are quick and easy to produce in a hurry, a filling option for big appetites and can be frozen if not used (space allowing).
- Packets of custard powder can be made quickly. Serve smaller amounts of the dessert and add extra custard. Some people enjoy custard on its own or with freshly sliced bananas to make a banana custard.

Essential equipment

- [ ] Large saucepans
- [ ] Large frying pans
- [ ] Large ovenproof dishes
- [ ] Large mixing bowls
- [ ] Large heatproof glass bowls
- [ ] Paring knives
- [ ] Bread knives
- [ ] Wooden spoons
- [ ] Tablespoons
- [ ] Teaspoons
- [ ] Potato mashers
- [ ] Cheese graters
- [ ] Pastry brushes
- [ ] Ice cream scoops
- [ ] Serving spoons
- [ ] Fish slices—useful for more than just fish!
- [ ] Soup ladles
- [ ] Measuring cups
- [ ] Measuring jugs
- [ ] Scales
- [ ] Electric whisk or hand whisk
- [ ] Electric hand-held blender
- [ ] Tin opener

- [ ] Kettle of boiled water—always good to have on hand
- [ ] Wipe-clean boards for chopping vegetables
- [ ] Wipe-clean boards for cooked meat
- [ ] Wipe-clean boards for raw meat
- [ ] Rolling pins
- [ ] Sieve
- [ ] Pastry cutters
- [ ] Baking sheets
- [ ] Pizza trays
- [ ] Catering-size clingfilm
- [ ] Catering-size cooking foil
- [ ] Kitchen paper
- [ ] Paper napkins
- [ ] A plentiful supply of clean tea towels (wash after each session)
- [ ] Disposable dishcloths (discard after each session)
- [ ] Washing-up liquid
- [ ] Dishwasher tablets
- [ ] Antibacterial kitchen cleaner
- [ ] Liquid hand soap
- [ ] Baby wet wipes (they have numerous uses)

All recipes will feed a family of four or five people

Shepherd's pie

Ingredients

- 1 tbsp oil
- 1 large onion, chopped
- 500g minced lamb
- 1 tbsp tomato puree (optional)
- 2 carrots, chopped
- 1 stock cube dissolved in ¾ pint of boiling water
- 2 tsps cornflour
- Cooked vegetables such as baked beans or tinned kidney beans (optional)
- 1kg potatoes
- Salt and pepper
- A little milk and margarine or butter to mash

Method

1. Fry onion in the oil until lightly browned. Add mince to the pan and continue to fry.
2. Add tomato puree, if using, and chopped carrots to pan.
3. Add stock cube dissolved in water, then bring mixture to the boil.
4. Simmer for 30 minutes until the mince is cooked.
5. Add a little cold water to the cornflour and mix to a pouring paste. Add to the meat mixture to thicken it. Season to taste.
6. At this stage, you could add other cooked vegetables such as baked beans or tinned kidney beans.
7. When cooked, strain as much of the gravy as possible from the meat mixture and place the meat in an ovenproof dish. Reserve the gravy to add to the finished dish.
8. Peel and cut up the potatoes into evenly sized pieces. Boil until tender (for approximately 15–20 minutes).
9. Strain the cooked potatoes and mash with a little milk and some butter or margarine to make them creamy. Season well.
10. Spread the potato over the meat until it is completely covered. Then dot the top of the potato with a little more margarine before placing in the oven to heat through and brown at 180°C or gas mark 4. This should take approximately 40 minutes.
11. Serve with the reserved gravy and any other vegetables of your choice.

Cook's tips

This dish freezes really well. Cool it quickly and cover with foil or clingfilm. Place in the freezer. When ready to use, defrost thoroughly and then reheat until it is piping hot in the middle of the dish. This should take approximately 40 minutes.

Cook's notes

Variations

- Vegetarian option: Use Quorn mince instead of meat.
- Cottage pie: Use beef mince instead of lamb.
- Cheesy shepherd's pie: Add some grated cheese on top of the potato before putting it in the oven.
- For a variation on the topping, use half potato and half parsnip or butternut squash to mash together.

Chilli con carne with nachos and cheese

Ingredients

- 1 tbsp oil
- 1 onion, chopped
- 2–4 cloves garlic, crushed
- 500g minced beef
- ½ tsp chilli powder (less or more if preferred)
- 1 tsp ground cumin (less if preferred)
- 400g can chopped tomatoes
- 1 beef stock cube
- ½ tsp dried oregano
- 1 tsp dried parsley or coriander
- 3 bay leaves
- Salt and pepper
- 400g can kidney beans
- 1 small square plain chocolate (over 70% solids)

Method

1. Put onion and crushed garlic into a pan and gently fry in the oil until soft. Add the mince and continue to fry until browned all over.
2. Add the chilli and cumin and stir well.
3. Add the tomatoes, stock cube (crumbled), herbs and seasoning and allow to cook, covered with a lid, for 20 minutes, adding a little more water if necessary.
4. Add the kidney beans and heat through well.
5. Finally, add the chocolate and make sure it dissolves properly.
6. Serve with a green salad, grated cheese, nachos and rice.

Cook's tips

The chocolate really does enrich the chilli but it is not essential. This dish freezes very well so can be made in advance.

Cook's notes

Variations

You could also serve this dish in a heated tortilla wrap with a dollop of sour cream, crème fraîche or thick yoghurt.

Pasta bolognaise

Ingredients

- 1 tbsp oil
- 1 large onion, chopped
- 2 garlic cloves, crushed
- 500g minced beef
- 1 tbsp tomato puree
- 400g can chopped tomatoes
- 1 red pepper, chopped
- 1 tsp dried basil
- 1 tsp dried oregano
- 3 bay leaves
- 1 stock cube dissolved in ¼ pint of boiling water
- 225g pasta shapes
- Salt and pepper
- Grated cheese

Method

1. Fry the onion in the oil until lightly browned. Add the garlic to the pan and fry. Add the beef and brown.
2. Add the tomato puree and then stir in the tomatoes, red pepper and herbs. Add stock cube dissolved in water, and then bring mixture to the boil.
3. Simmer the mixture for 30 minutes. It is even nicer to simmer for longer, as long as you add a little water to stop it drying out. Season well.
4. Cook the pasta as directed on the packet.
5. Serve the pasta with the meat and with some grated cheese on top.

Cook's tips

- Add some mushrooms if you like them.
- The garlic is optional, so remove if you don't like it or add some more if you do!
- The dish can be made with other types of mince as well as beef.

Variations

For a vegetarian option, use chopped aubergine instead of meat.

Cook's notes

Pasta with tomato and basil sauce

Ingredients

- 50g butter
- 50ml olive oil
- 1 onion, chopped
- 400g can chopped tomatoes
- 50g tomato puree
- ½ tsp sugar
- Salt and pepper
- Dried basil (to taste)
- 225g pasta shapes
- 225g grated cheese
- French bread or bread rolls

Method

1. Gently heat the butter and oil in a pan. Add the onion and fry gently until softened and transparent.
2. Add tomatoes, tomato puree, sugar, salt and pepper. Bring slowly to the boil, stirring occasionally.
3. Turn heat down to simmer, uncovered, for 40–50 minutes. Then liquidise the mixture.
4. Stir in the basil and adjust seasoning.
5. Cook the pasta as instructed on the packet.
6. Drain the pasta and stir into the sauce. Re-heat, and stir in grated cheese.
7. Serve with French bread or bread rolls.

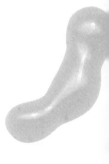

Cook's tips

- Slow cookers are useful to keep the sauce hot.
- This recipe is ideal for the first week, when numbers attending are uncertain. Keep back some sauce with an extra packet of pasta in case extra people turn up. If there are no extra people, stir the sauce into the pasta to be served.
- Have some plain pasta available for children who don't like the sauce.

Variations

Use fresh basil instead of dried.

Cook's notes

Flash-in-the-pan sausages

Ingredients

- 1 tbsp oil
- 8 pork sausages
- 1 small onion, chopped
- 400g can cannellini beans, drained and rinsed
- 400g can chopped tomatoes
- 1 tbsp golden syrup
- 2 tsp Worcestershire sauce (or HP brown sauce or a dash of Tabasco sauce for a really hot and spicy taste)
- Hot water

Method

1. Heat the oil in a large frying pan and fry the sausages over a medium heat for 20 minutes, turning them now and again. Remove sausages from the pan and set aside.
2. Add chopped onion to the pan and cook for 3–4 minutes. Tip in the beans and tomatoes, stir through and cook for 2–3 minutes.
3. Add golden syrup and either of the sauces you are using. Also add ¼ pint of hot water and stir well.
4. Return the sausages to the pan to heat through until all the sauce is bubbling.

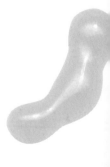

Cook's tips

Serve this dish with mashed potato.

Variations

- Use canned kidney beans instead of cannellini beans.
- For a vegetarian option, use vegetarian sausages, cooked as per instructions on the pack.

Cook's notes

Frankfurter Jambalaya

Ingredients

- 2 chicken or vegetarian stock cubes
- Boiling water
- 1 tbsp oil
- 1 onion, chopped
- 2 cloves garlic, chopped
- 3 cups long-grain rice
- 1 packet of ten vacuum-packed frankfurters
- 6 mushrooms, cooked
- 1 packet frozen mixed vegetables, cooked
- Handful of fresh chopped parsley
- French bread or garlic bread

Method

1. Dissolve the stock cubes in six cups of boiling water.
2. Put oil into a deep-sided frying pan or large saucepan. Add onion and chopped garlic and fry until soft and just beginning to brown. Add the washed rice and stir, frying gently for 2–3 minutes.
3. Gradually add stock, stirring all the time, allowing rice to cook. You may need to add a little more water.
4. Heat frankfurters in boiling water for the time stated on the packet. Then cut them into bite-sized pieces. Add to the cooked rice with mushrooms, mixed vegetables and parsley. Stir thoroughly and reheat if necessary.
5. Serve with lots of French bread or garlic bread.

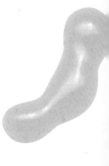

Cook's tips

To make the meat stretch a little bit further, make a two-egg omelette and, when it is cooked, cut into pieces and add to the rice as well.

Variations

Instead of frankfurters, you could use leftover roast chicken and/or chopped ham.

Cook's notes

Roast turkey and trimmings

Ingredients

- 1 small whole turkey, a turkey crown, or four fillet pieces (a mixture of legs and breast)
- Olive oil, salt and pepper
- 450g potatoes
- 8 chipolata sausages
- 8 rashers of streaky bacon
- Seasonal mixed vegetables
- 1 small onion, finely chopped
- 110g fresh breadcrumbs (brown or white)
- A knob of butter
- 1 tsp dried mixed herbs
- 1 chicken stock cube dissolved in ¼ pint of boiling water
- 2 tsps cornflour

Method

1. Place the turkey in a roasting dish, drizzle with olive oil and season to taste. Cover with foil and cook by following the directions on the label. The meat must be cooked through until the juices run clear when pierced with a knife. Undercooking is a food poisoning risk, but try not to overcook, as this will make the meat more difficult to carve.

2. Peel or wipe the potatoes and cut into pieces of even size. Parboil for 10 minutes. Drain and place in a roasting dish. Drizzle with oil and roast at 220°C or gas mark 7 for 40–50 minutes, or until golden brown.

3. Separate the chipolata sausages and wrap each chipolata in bacon. Place in a roasting tin and drizzle with oil. Roast at 220°C or gas mark 7 for 40–50 minutes.

4. Peel, clean and chop the vegetables. Fill a saucepan with water to a depth of about 5cm and bring to the boil. Place vegetables in the water and bring back to the boil. Simmer for 10–20 minutes until tender.

5. Cook the chopped onion in some water until it begins to get soft. Mix together with the breadcrumbs and add a knob of butter, some mixed herbs and seasoning.

6. Moisten the mixture with some of the onion water, then roll into balls and bake at 190°C or gas mark 5 for 20–30 minutes.

7. Make the gravy by adding the dissolved stock cube to the vegetable water. Add the meat juices after removing most of the fat.

8. Mix the cornflour with a little water and stir into the gravy, bring gently to the boil and stir while the mixture thickens slightly.

Cook's tips

- If you don't want to make fresh stuffing, use a packet stuffing of your choice and follow the instructions on the packet.
- If you don't want to make gravy from scratch, use instant gravy granules and follow the instructions on the packet.
- As an extra festive touch, cranberry sauce can be served on the side.

Cook's notes

Variations

For a vegetarian option, use Quorn steaks, and serve with vegetarian sausages. Use vegetable stock to make the gravy.

Crispy turkey bites

Ingredients

- 500g turkey breast
- Juice of one lemon
- 2 cloves garlic, crushed (optional)
- Black pepper
- Pinch of salt
- Plain flour, seasoned (to coat)
- 2 eggs (beaten)
- Dried or fresh breadcrumbs

Method

1. Cut turkey breasts into 2cm cubes.
2. Allow to marinate for at least one hour in the lemon juice, crushed garlic and salt and pepper.
3. Shake surplus liquid from the turkey.
4. Put seasoned flour in a bowl. Add the pieces of turkey and coat well. Shake off surplus flour.
5. Put beaten eggs into a bowl and add turkey pieces a few at a time. Drain them through your fingers and put them straight into the breadcrumbs to coat. At this stage you could freeze them by putting on a baking sheet lined with greaseproof paper. Open freeze for four hours; then, when solid, place into freezer bags or boxes.
6. To cook from frozen, preheat oven to 220°C or gas mark 7. Pour a little oil on to a baking sheet and allow it to get hot in the oven. Then place the turkey bites on to the baking sheet and cook for approximately 15 minutes until cooked through.
7. To cook from chilled, reduce cooking time to approximately 10 minutes. Always check that chicken is cooked through, and adjust cooking time if necessary.

Cook's tips

- Make sure the turkey is cooked through, as ovens do vary in temperature.
- You can also deep-fry the turkey, which will take a little less time.
- Breadcrumbs are easy to make and are an economical way to use up bread (brown or white, and crusts too). Just lay sliced bread on to baking sheets and slowly bake in the oven at 130°C or gas mark 2 until crisp but not browned. You can then place them into an electric or hand grinder to make the crumbs, or you can place between a folded clean tea towel and bash with a rolling pin. (Great for releasing tension!) These breadcrumbs will keep for several weeks in an airtight container.

Variations

Use chicken breast instead of turkey.

Cook's notes

Mixed beef and vegetable pie

Ingredients

- 1 large onion, chopped
- 500g minced beef
- 2 stock cubes dissolved in 1 pint of water
- ½ tsp mixed herbs
- 2 carrots, diced
- 4 tbsp swede, diced
- 4 tbsp frozen peas
- 2 tsp cornflour
- Water and seasoning

For the pastry:

- 500g plain flour
- 250g margarine, or margarine and lard in a 50–50 mixture
- Pinch of salt
- 4–5 tbsp cold water
- 1 beaten egg

Method

1. Fry the onion until soft. Add meat to the pan and brown well.
2. Add stock and herbs and cook until the meat is tender.
3. Add carrots and swede and cook until tender.
4. Add frozen peas and cook for a further five minutes before seasoning.
5. Mix the cornflour with a little cold water and mix. Add to the meat and reboil the mixture so that it thickens slightly.
6. Drain the meat from the gravy and allow to cool.
7. To make the pastry, rub the fat into the flour and salt until it resembles fine breadcrumbs. Add 4 tablespoons of water and mix to form a dough. Add a little more water if necessary. Do not knead the dough but just work it lightly.
8. To make the pie, roll out just over half of the pastry, and line a dinner plate or a similar shallow ovenproof dish with it.
9. Fill the pastry with the cooked meat.
10. Roll out the rest of the pastry and place it on top of the meat, after moistening the edges of the pie with some beaten egg. Make sure the edges are sealed well. Cut two slits in the top of the pie with the point of a knife and then brush it with the rest of the egg.
11. Cook at 200°C or gas mark 6 for 20–30 minutes, until golden brown.
12. Serve the pie with vegetables and the rest of the gravy.

Cook's tips

- Make sure the meat is cooked before adding vegetables.
- Halve the ingredients for the pastry and omit lining the dish with pastry— just add the pastry crust.

Variations

- Use diced beef instead of minced beef, or diced lamb instead of beef.
- For a vegetarian option, use Quorn chunks instead of meat.

Cook's notes

Winter hotpot

Ingredients

- 1 large onion, chopped
- 500g diced lamb
- 2 stock cubes dissolved in 570ml of water
- 2 cloves of garlic, peeled and chopped
- 2 tbsp tomato puree
- 1 tsp dried basil
- 1 tsp dried oregano
- 3 bay leaves
- Handful fresh chopped parsley
- 2 carrots, diced
- 4 tbsp swede, diced
- 4 tbsp turnip, diced
- 4 tbsp frozen peas
- 2 tsp cornflour
- Water
- 225g long-grain rice
- Seasoning

Method

1. Fry the onion until soft. Add meat to the pan and brown well.
2. Add stock, garlic, tomato puree and herbs, and cook until the meat is tender.
3. Add carrots, swede and turnip, and cook until the vegetables are tender.
4. Add frozen peas and cook for a further five minutes before seasoning.
5. Mix the cornflour with a little cold water and mix. Add to the pan and reboil the mixture so that it thickens slightly.
6. In a separate pan, cook the rice in boiling water according to the instructions on the packet.
7. Serve the hotpot on a bed of rice.

Cook's tips

- For extra tomato flavour, add a 400g can of chopped tomatoes.
- For added comfort eating, serve with French bread or garlic bread.

Cook's notes

Variations

- Use diced beef instead of lamb.
- For a vegetarian option, omit the meat and add one diced aubergine, one diced red pepper and a 400g can of mixed beans.
- Serve with mashed potato or baked potatoes instead of rice.

Sausage rolls

Ingredients

- 500g shop-bought puff or shortcrust pastry
- 500g good-quality sausagemeat
- Flour
- 1 egg (beaten)

Method

1. Roll out the pastry into an oblong shape.
2. Roll the sausagemeat into two long lengths, using a little flour to stop it sticking.
3. Place the sausagemeat lengths on top of the pastry and cut pastry in half down the middle.
4. Brush some beaten egg along one length of each piece of pastry.
5. Roll the pastry up, wrapping the sausagemeat inside and making sure that the edges are sealed.
6. Cut little nicks in the top of the pastry to let the air escape, brush with some more beaten egg and then cut each long length into smaller rolls.
7. Place on a greased baking sheet and cook for approximately 20 minutes at 200°C or gas mark 6.

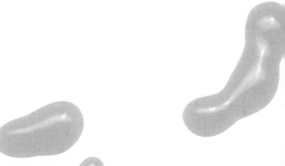

Cook's tips

- Serve with tinned tomatoes, baked beans or sweetcorn.
- Provide tomato ketchup or relish on the side.

Cook's notes

Variations

For a different taste, add one of the following to the sausagemeat:
- 1 tsp dried sage
- ½ tsp chilli pepper (no more!)
- 50g grated cheese and a little mustard

Sausage pie

Ingredients

- 300g shortcrust pastry
- 500g pork sausagemeat
- 1 tsp dried sage
- A little beaten egg for glazing

Method

1. Roll out half of the pastry and line a pie dish or deep sided plate.
2. Mix sausagemeat in a bowl with a fork and stir in sage.
3. Spread sausage mixture on to pastry. Moisten the edges and place the other half of rolled-out pastry on top. Crimp the edges and make two cuts on top of the pastry with a knife to let the steam escape.
4. Glaze with beaten egg.
5. Cook in a pre-heated oven for 20 minutes at 200°C or gas mark 6. Then turn down oven to 180°C or gas mark 4 and continue to cook for a further 30 minutes.

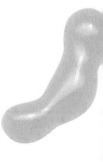

Cook's tips

This pie is delicious served with baked beans and mashed potato, but equally smashing served cold with salads and pickles.

Cook's notes

Variations

- Other ideas are to grate some cheese on top of the sausagemeat, then put either cooked sliced onion or drained tinned tomatoes on top, before the pastry lid, and cook.
- To make a lovely picnic pie, lightly boil three eggs for six minutes, carefully take off the shells and bury them in the sausagemeat. Finish the pie and bake.

45

Chicken casserole

Ingredients

- 800g diced chicken breast or boned chicken thighs
- 2 tbsp plain flour
- A little butter or oil
- 2 medium onions, chopped
- 500g carrots, diced
- 1 stick celery, chopped
- 2 cloves garlic, crushed
- 1 tbsp tomato puree
- 2 stock cubes dissolved in 1½ pints of water
- 1 tbsp herbs de Provence or mixed herbs
- 1 green or red pepper (finely chopped)

Method

1. Coat the chicken in the flour and fry in the butter or oil until golden in colour. Remove from the pan.
2. Add the onion, carrots and celery to the pan and fry for five minutes until slightly soft. Add the garlic and put the chicken back into the pan.
3. Add the tomato puree and then stir in the stock, herbs and chopped pepper.
4. Bring everything to the boil and simmer for one hour.

Cook's tips

Other vegetables can be added to the casserole—mushrooms are particularly tasty.

Variations

For a vegetarian option, replace the chicken with Quorn chunks and use vegetable stock instead of chicken.

Cook's notes

Chicken and vegetable cobbler

Ingredients

- 4 chicken breasts
- A little oil
- 1 onion, chopped
- 1 leek, sliced
- 2 cloves garlic, chopped
- 1 tbsp flour
- 1 tbsp tomato puree
- 2 chicken stock cubes
- 1½ pints boiling water
- 250g frozen mixed vegetables

For the cobbler:

- 225g self-raising flour
- Pinch of salt and pepper
- 50g margarine
- 1 tsp of mixed herbs or parsley
- Cold milk to mix

Method

1. Cut chicken into cubes.
2. Fry onion, leek and garlic in oil until soft and beginning to turn brown.
3. In a separate pan, fry chicken until beginning to turn a golden colour.
4. Add the chicken to the onion and leek. Sprinkle flour over the chicken and onion and stir until flour is incorporated into the oil.
5. Add tomato puree and stir well.
6. Crumble stock cubes into boiling water and stir into the chicken mixture until it begins to thicken slightly.
7. Add the mixed vegetables and cook until chicken is tender. Check seasoning.

For the cobbler:

1. Sift flour into a bowl with the salt and pepper.
2. Rub in the margarine, and then stir in the mixed herbs or parsley.
3. Add enough cold milk to form a soft dough.
4. Roll out on a floured board to 1½ cm and cut with round or square cutters.
5. Put chicken into an ovenproof dish and lay the cobblers on top. Brush with milk and cook in the oven at 200°C or gas mark 6 for 25–30 minutes, or until golden and well risen.

Cook's tips

A cobbler topping is delicious on any other type of casserole or even a savoury mince.

Variations

For a vegetarian option, replace the chicken with Quorn chunks and use vegetable stock instead of chicken.

Cook's notes

All-in-one corned beef casserole

Ingredients

- 1 tbsp oil
- 4 potatoes, peeled and chopped
- 2 onions, peeled and chopped
- 4 carrots, peeled and chopped
- 2 stock cubes
- ½ pint boiling water
- 2 tins corned beef

Method

1. Place oil in a large pan and heat gently.
2. Add the chopped potatoes, onions and carrots to the pan and stir. Cook until starting to soften, stirring occasionally.
3. Dissolve the stock cubes in boiling water.
4. Chop the corned beef and add to the vegetables with the dissolved stock cubes.
5. Bring to the boil and simmer gently until everything is heated through.

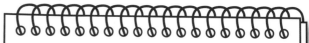

Cook's tips

Add additional vegetables that are in season.

Variations

Replace the stock with a tin of chopped tomatoes for a different flavour.

Cook's notes

Corned beef hash

Ingredients

- 1 tbsp oil
- 1 onion, peeled and chopped
- 1 tin corned beef, chopped
- Salt and pepper
- 3 baking size potatoes, boiled until soft, and mashed

Method

1. Pour a little oil into a large pan.
2. Add the chopped onion and cook until softened, stirring occasionally.
3. Stir in the chopped corned beef.
4. Season as desired.
5. Mix in the potato and heat through thoroughly before serving.

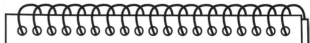

Cook's tips

Add a tin of chopped tomatoes to make the recipe stretch further.

Variations

Add other vegetables, such as mushrooms, in season. Alternatively, add more vegetables, omit the potatoes and top with pastry to make a corned beef pie.

Cook's notes

Broccoli, cheese and pasta bake

Ingredients

- 1 small head of broccoli, washed and cut into small florets
- 100g penne pasta
- 50g butter or margarine
- 50g plain flour
- 1 pint milk, heated to just boiling
- 125g cheddar cheese
- 1 tsp ready-made mustard seasoning
- 2 tomatoes, sliced
- 2 packets of plain crisps, crushed

Method

1. Cook broccoli in boiling water for five minutes. Drain and leave aside.
2. Cook pasta until just soft (do not overcook at this stage as it is cooked further in the oven).
3. Melt the butter or margarine in a pan and add the flour. Mix with a wooden spoon to form a roux.
4. Gradually whisk in the heated milk to make a coating sauce. Once thickened, use a wooden spoon to continue stirring.
5. Remove sauce from the heat and add half of the cheese and the mustard.
6. After straining the pasta, place in an ovenproof dish. Add the broccoli and then pour the sauce over.
7. Arrange sliced tomato on top. Mix the remaining cheese with the crushed crisps and sprinkle all over the top.
8. Cook in the oven at 180°C or gas mark 4 until golden on top.

Cook's tips

Use different shaped pasta, such as twists, bows or macaroni.

Cook's notes

Variations

Add cooked mushrooms and diced ham to the pasta instead of broccoli.

Tuna pasta

Ingredients

- 1 vegetable stock cube dissolved in ½ pint water
- 1 stick celery, chopped
- 1 onion, chopped
- 100g pasta twists
- 400g chopped tomatoes
- 1 tbsp tomato puree
- 4 tbsp cooked peas
- 4 tbsp cooked sweetcorn
- 1 tsp mixed herbs
- 1 tsp granulated sugar
- 1 large tin of tuna
- Salt and pepper

Method

1. Cook the chopped celery and onion in the stock for 30 minutes until the liquid has reduced by half.
2. Cook the pasta twists according to the instructions on the packet.
3. Add tomatoes, tomato puree, peas and sweetcorn to the celery and onion and heat through. Add the herbs.
4. Add the sugar to the mixture. Season to taste, then mix in the tuna. Heat through but do not overcook.
5. Pour tuna mixture over the cooked pasta twists.

Cook's tips

If you don't have tomato puree on hand, substitute with tomato ketchup and omit the sugar.

Cook's notes

Variations

- Top with crushed crisps and bake in the oven until golden.
- Replace the pasta with couscous. Allow 50g dry couscous per person. Soak in hot stock using the measurements on the packet.
- Replace the tuna with frankfurter sausages. Heat the sausages according to instructions on the packet and then chop them and stir into the dish at the final stage. Allow two or three sausages per person, depending on appetites.

Meatballs in tomato and green pepper sauce

Ingredients

- 500g beef mince
- 250g pork mince
- 2 slices bread, made into breadcrumbs
- 1 onion, finely chopped
- 1 clove garlic
- 1 tsp dried oregano
- 1 tsp dried parsley
- 1 dsp tomato puree
- 1 egg, beaten
- Seasoning
- Flour to coat balls
- Oil for frying

For the sauce

- 1 onion, chopped
- 1 clove garlic, crushed
- ½ green pepper, sliced
- 400g chopped tomatoes
- 1 tsp basil (fresh or dried)
- 1 beef stock cube dissolved in ½ pint water
- Seasoning

Method

1. For the meatballs, mix together the two meats, add the breadcrumbs, onion, garlic, herbs, tomato puree and beaten egg. Combine together well and add seasoning.
2. Coating with flour, form the mixture into balls the size of a walnut. Fry them in oil to brown all over. Remove from pan and set aside.
3. For the sauce, fry the onion in the pan, add crushed garlic and green pepper and cook for one minute.
4. Add tomatoes, basil and beef stock, then season.
5. Put the meatballs in an ovenproof dish, pour over the sauce and cook at 180°C or gas mark 4 for 40–45 minutes.

Cook's tips

Serve with seasonal vegetables, rice or spaghetti.

Variations

For a vegetarian option, use minced Quorn instead of the beef and pork.

Cook's notes

Fish cakes

Ingredients

- 400g filleted white fish (coley, cod or haddock)
- A little milk
- 325g potatoes, peeled and cut into even sized pieces (King Edward or Maris Piper are best)
- Salt and pepper
- 25g butter
- A good handful of chopped fresh parsley (dried will do, but only use 2 tsp)
- 1 egg, beaten
- Flour for dusting
- A little oil for shallow frying
- Lemon wedges

Method

1. Cook fish gently in milk in a covered saucepan for about 6–8 minutes. Do not overcook at this stage.
2. Allow fish to cool and then drain well.
3. Meanwhile, boil potatoes until soft. Drain well and mash. Add seasoning and butter.
4. Flake the fish and remove any bones or skin. Add to the potatoes with parsley and beaten egg.
5. Put some seasoned flour on to a board. Flour hands and mould the fish mixture into flat cakes.
6. Shallow fry until golden on each side. Serve with lemon wedges.

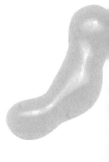

Cook's tips

Pin bone the fish before cooking and check again for any remaining bones when you flake the fish. In white fish, the bones always lie between the flakes.

Cook's notes

Variations

Fish cakes are lovely served with a homemade tartar sauce, which is easy to make as follows:

- 4 tbsp good mayonnaise
- 2 tsp snipped chives
- 1 tbsp chopped gherkin
- 1 tbsp capers
- 1 tbsp chopped parsley
- 1–2 tsp lemon juice

Combine all the ingredients and serve.

Another alternative is to replace the white fish with tinned tuna or salmon, allowing one 213g tin per two people.

July

Quick chicken surprise

Ingredients

- 1 tin condensed chicken soup
- 2 tbsp mayonnaise
- 1 stick celery, finely chopped
- 500g cold cooked chicken, off the bone
- 2 hardboiled eggs
- 2 packets of plain crisps, crushed
- Seasoning

Method

1. Place soup and mayonnaise in a bowl and mix together well.
2. Stir in the celery and chicken, and season.
3. Quarter the eggs and place in the bottom of an ovenproof dish. Then spread the chicken mixture on top.
4. Liberally cover the top with the crushed crisps.
5. Cook in the oven at 180°C or gas mark 4 for 30–40 minutes.

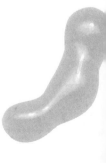

Cook's tips

Serve with salad and French bread.

Cook's notes

Variations

Use turkey or Quorn chunks instead of chicken. Replace the chicken soup with cream of mushroom soup.

Easy chicken and ham pie

Ingredients

- 1 medium chicken
- 1 chicken stock cube, crumbled
- 1 onion, chopped
- 1 carrot, chopped
- 1 stick of celery, chopped
- Salt and pepper
- 25g margarine or butter
- 25g plain flour
- 250g shortcrust pastry
- A little beaten egg
- 100g chopped ham
- 50g frozen peas, cooked
- 50g frozen sweetcorn, cooked

Method

1. Put chicken into saucepan and just cover with water. Add the crumbled stock cube, onion, carrot, celery and seasoning.
2. Bring to the boil and cook, covered, for 50 minutes. Remove the cooked chicken from the liquid and put aside to cool. Strain one pint of the stock into a jug.
3. Melt margarine or butter in a saucepan and add the flour. Mix with a wooden spoon to make a roux. Now gradually add the stock, beating well to avoid lumps. This will make a pouring sauce.
4. Roll out pastry and cut into triangles or other interesting shapes. Place on a greased baking sheet and brush with egg. Bake at 200°C or gas mark 6 until golden. Set aside.
5. Remove the chicken from the bones and cut into smaller pieces. Add the chicken, ham, peas and sweetcorn to the sauce, heating well. If it is a bit too thick, add some milk or cream. Taste and season. Pour into a shallow dish, place cooked pastry on top, and serve.

Cook's tips

- Puff pastry is a delicious alternative to shortcrust pastry.
- If your family or group doesn't like the chicken in a white sauce, you could always thicken the chicken stock with chicken gravy powder to make a brown gravy.
- Use shaped biscuit cutters to cut out pastry shapes to go on top of the pie. The shapes could match your Messy Church theme, such as lion shapes for the story of Daniel in the lions' den, and various animal shapes for the story of creation or Noah's ark.

Cook's notes

Variations

Instead of sweetcorn, you could add some cooked mushrooms. If you prefer to make a proper pie, just place the rolled-out pastry on top of the chicken, sealing the edges well, and cook for 20–30 minutes in the oven at 200°C or gas mark 6.

Walking tacos

Ingredients

- 4 individual small packets of tortilla chips (such as Doritos)
- 4 tbsp chilli con carne (see recipe on page 24)
- 1 little gem lettuce, shredded
- 4 tomatoes, chopped
- 4 tsp ready-made salsa

Method

1. Invite each person to open their bag of tortilla chips and hold the neck of the bag firmly.
2. Crush the tortilla chips inside the bag.
3. Open the bag and spoon a handful of lettuce, one chopped tomato, one tbsp chilli con carne and 1 tsp salsa (optional) into the bag.
4. Hold the neck of bag and gently shake the contents.
5. Open the bag, take a fork and enjoy.

Cook's tips

- To prevent tortilla chips going soggy, make sure the chilli doesn't have too much extra liquid.
- Use this recipe when you want to cut down on the washing up!

Variations

- Add grated cheese or sour cream if desired.
- For a vegetarian alternative, use Quorn chilli or chilli spiced mixed beans.

Cook's notes

Sitting tacos

Ingredients

- Taco shells (the taco trays are best if you can get them), enough for three per adult and two per child
- 4 tbsp chilli con carne (see recipe on page 24)
- 1 little gem lettuce, shredded
- 4 tomatoes, chopped
- 4 tsp ready-made salsa

Method

1. Place the shells or trays, open side down, in a hot oven (to prevent them closing).
2. Invite each person to spoon in a serving of lettuce, tomato, chilli and salsa (optional).
3. Serve in paper napkins or sheets of kitchen roll. (The tacos will crumble but that's half of the fun!)

Cook's tips

- The secret is not to overfill the tacos, but have plenty of paper napkins or kitchen roll to hand.
- Heat the shells in a microwave instead of a conventional oven.

Variations

- Add grated cheese or sour cream if desired.
- For a vegetarian alternative, use Quorn mince or chilli spiced mixed beans.

Cook's notes

All recipes will feed a family of four or five people

Yorkshire pudding dessert

Ingredients

- 175g plain flour
- Pinch of salt
- 2 eggs
- Half a pint of milk
- A little oil for cooking
- Handful of currants and jam (any flavour)

Method

1. Sift the flour and salt into a bowl. Make a well in the centre and put the eggs and one-third of the milk into the centre.
2. Stir well with a whisk, gradually incorporating the flour from the sides to make a thick batter. Beat well.
3. Gradually add the remaining milk. Beat well and leave to stand for one hour.
4. Add the currants and mix well. Pre-heat oven to 220°C, gas mark 7. Spoon oil into small patty tins and place tins in the oven to get the oil hot.
5. Pour the batter into a jug, remove patty tins from oven and immediately pour batter into tins. Place in the oven and cook for approximately 10–12 minutes, until well risen and puffy.
6. Serve immediately with the jam on the table so that everyone can spoon it on to their pudding.

Cook's tips

Always use plain flour for this recipe. Self-raising flour will not allow the puddings to puff up.

Variations

Serve with squeezy golden syrup instead of jam.

Easy option

Ice cream with marshmallows and squeezy chocolate and raspberry sauces.

Cook's notes

Chocolate pudding with chocolate sauce

Ingredients

- 125g caster sugar
- 100g self-raising flour
- 25g cocoa powder
- 1 tsp baking powder
- 125g soft margarine
- 1 tbsp water
- 2 medium eggs, beaten

For the sauce

- 1 tin or carton of ready-made custard
- 100g plain chocolate, grated

Method

1. To make the pudding, sift all the dry ingredients together and place into a mixing bowl.
2. Add the other ingredients and beat with an electric mixer for two minutes only. You could use a wooden spoon but it will take longer.
3. Spoon the mixture into a greased ovenproof dish and bake in the oven for 15 minutes at 180°C or gas mark 4.
4. To make the sauce, heat the custard in a saucepan, stirring all the time until it is just bubbling.
5. Add the grated chocolate and stir through. For a darker sauce, just add more chocolate.

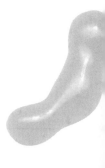

Cook's tips

The pudding can be cooked in a microwave. Place the mixture in a greased pudding basin and cook on full power for about 4–5 minutes. This is great fun to watch, but don't leave it cooking on its own as timings can vary!

Variations

Omit the cocoa powder from the pudding and add 2 tsp ground ginger. Serve with squeezy golden syrup instead of chocolate sauce.

Easy option

Serve grapes and bananas.

Cook's notes

Butterscotch tart

Ingredients

- 200g shortcrust pastry
- 150g butter
- 150g soft brown sugar
- 3½ fluid oz milk and 3 level tbsps flour blended together

Method

1. Roll out pastry and line a flan tin or dish. Prick the base and bake blind in the oven at 200°C or gas mark 6 for 15–20 minutes, until crisp.
2. Place all the ingredients for the filling into a thick-bottomed saucepan and bring slowly to the boil. Cook for 2–3 minutes, stirring all the time, until the mixture thickens. Pour into pastry case and leave to cool and set. Serve with whipped cream or ice cream.

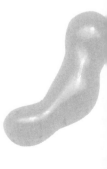

Cook's tips

To save time, you could use a ready-made pastry case from the supermarket.

Variations

Crush a chocolate flake over the top.

Easy option

Fruit flan with cream.

Cook's notes

Mince tart

Ingredients

- 200g shortcrust pastry
- 454g jar mincemeat
- Icing sugar
- Single cream

Method

You will need star-shaped pastry cutters.

1. Roll out the pastry to line a 20cm flan dish.
2. Spread the mincemeat evenly in the lined dish.
3. Cut star shapes from leftover pastry and place on the mincemeat.
4. Bake in the oven at 200°C or gas mark 6 for 25–30 minutes, or until the pastry is golden brown and the mincemeat cooked through.
5. Allow to cool before sifting the icing sugar over the top.
6. Slice and serve with cream.

Cook's tips

Mince tart is also very good served with vanilla ice cream.

Variations

- Peel and core a cooking apple, finely slice and arrange in the bottom of the pastry case before adding the mincemeat.
- As an alternative to topping the tart with pastry stars, slice an orange or satsuma across the width to form a circle shape showing the segments and place in the centre. Surround the orange with mincemeat. Cover the orange circle with foil while baking. When cool, sprinkle the tart with icing sugar and then remove the foil to produce a festive tart with a snowy top and lovely festive orange scent and colour.

Easy option

Use ready-made mince pies or a mixture of mince pies and jam tarts served with cream.

Cook's notes

Lemon sponge

Ingredients

- 115g margarine
- 115g caster sugar
- 2 eggs, beaten
- 115g self-raising flour
- Margarine for greasing
- Grated rind and juice from one lemon
- Half a jar good-quality lemon curd
- 1 tbsp water

Method

1. Cream margarine and sugar together until light and fluffy.
2. Gradually add the beaten eggs.
3. Fold in the sifted flour and mix in the lemon juice and rind. If the mixture seems a little stiff, add a little water.
4. Grease an ovenproof dish with some margarine. Add the tablespoon of water to the lemon curd and mix well. Place this into the bottom of the greased dish, and spoon the sponge mix over it.
5. Place dish into a roasting tin and add boiling water to come halfway up the side of the dish. Carefully place in the oven and cook for approximately 30–40 minutes at 180°C or gas mark 5.
6. Serve with custard or cream.

Cook's tips

For a traditional shape, use a 1 pint ovenproof pudding basin.

Variations

Omit the lemon rind and juice and lemon curd, and place 2 tbsp squeezy golden syrup in the bottom of the dish or basin before adding the sponge mixture.

Easy option

Cakes and tray bakes.

Cook's notes

Apple crumble

Ingredients

- 2 large cooking apples, peeled and cored
- 2 tbsp granulated sugar for sprinkling
- Juice of one lemon or orange
- 200g plain flour
- ½ tsp cinnamon
- 100g margarine or butter
- 50g sugar

Method

1. Slice the apples thinly and place in an ovenproof dish.
2. Sprinkle with 2 tbsp sugar and then pour over the lemon or orange juice.
3. Sift the flour and cinnamon into a bowl and rub in the butter or margarine until it resembles fine breadcrumbs.
4. Stir in the 50g sugar.
5. Cover the apples completely with the crumble mixture and bake for approximately 40 minutes at 190°C or gas mark 5.
   If the top of the crumble starts to brown too quickly, just turn down the temperature a little.
6. Serve with custard or cream.

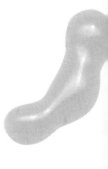

Cook's tips

- You could also replace 50g of the flour with some rolled oats or oatmeal for a more crunchy topping. Another idea is to add some sultanas or other dried fruit, such as dates, to the apple mixture.
- Use different fruit, such as rhubarb.

Variations

For a crumble topping with a difference, add one of the following after you have stirred in the sugar (step 4):
- the grated rind of one lemon or orange
- some ground ginger (especially nice if you use rhubarb instead of apple).

Easy option

Small pots of chocolate, caramel or fruit yogurts.

Cook's notes

Bread and butter pudding

Ingredients

- 1 pint milk
- 4 egg yolks, plus one more egg, beaten
- 115g sugar
- 6 slices of white bread, crusts removed
- 75g butter or margarine
- 50g sultanas
- Grated nutmeg
- A little extra Demerara sugar

Method

1. Heat the milk in the saucepan until almost boiling and then remove from heat. Pour on to the beaten yolks and egg and beat well together. Add sugar and mix.
2. Spread the bread with butter or margarine and cut into triangles. Place into a buttered ovenproof dish, overlapping the bread slightly and scattering the sultanas as you go.
3. Pour over the egg and milk mixture evenly and allow to soak for 20 minutes.
4. Meanwhile, preheat the oven to gas mark 5 or 180°C.
5. Sprinkle pudding with nutmeg and Demerara sugar, place the dish in a roasting tin and pour in enough boiling water to come halfway up the sides of the dish.
6. Bake in the centre of the oven for 40 minutes or until the custard is just set and the top is golden and crisp. Serve with cream or custard.

Cook's tips

For a special occasion and a richer pudding, you could use half milk and half cream to make the egg custard.

Variations

- You could also use other breads, such as brioche, panettone or fruit loaf.
- Cinnamon is another tasty spice you could use.

Easy option

Fruit yogurts.

Cook's notes

Fruit pavlova

Ingredients

- 4 egg whites
- 225g caster sugar
- 1 tsp cornflour
- 1 tsp white wine vinegar
- ½ tsp vanilla essence
- ½ pint double cream
- Fresh fruit of choice, such as raspberries, blueberries, pineapple, strawberries

Method

1. Preheat oven to 130°C or gas mark ½. Line a baking sheet with non-stick baking parchment and draw a 23cm or 9 inch circle on the paper. Turn the paper over.
2. Using a whisk (electric is best), whisk egg whites until they form soft peaks. While the whisk is still running, gradually add the sugar, a spoonful at a time. The meringue should become stiff and shiny.
3. Mix the cornflour, vinegar and vanilla essence together and add to the meringue with a metal spoon. Spoon on to the baking paper within the pencil circle, and then add spoonfuls of meringue around the edges to form a ring.
4. Bake for one hour and 30 minutes, or until dry and a little soft in the centre. Switch off the oven and leave the meringue to cool in the oven. Then transfer to a plate, removing the baking parchment.
5. Whip the cream until it forms soft peaks, fill the centre of the meringue with cream and then pile on the fruit.

Cook's tips

Freeze the leftover egg yolks by mixing with some caster sugar. Use approximately two teaspoons of caster sugar for four egg yolks. Then open-freeze in ice cube trays. When almost set but firm, pop them out and place into a freezer bag to continue to freeze. Each cube is approximately one egg yolk. Defrost well before using. Use them up to make bread and butter pudding (see page 84).

Variations

Use crème fraîche or low-fat Greek yoghurt instead of the cream.

Easy option

Brownie tray bake with crème fraîche.

Cook's notes

Jelly whip

Ingredients

- 1 packet of jelly (any flavour)
- ¼ pint boiling water
- 1 large tin evaporated milk (put this in the fridge first to get it really cold)

Method

1. Dissolve the jelly in the boiling water, and place in the fridge to cool until the jelly is just beginning to set.
2. Put the evaporated milk into a bowl and use an electric mixer to whisk until it is thick and creamy.
3. Whisk in the cold jelly, then pile immediately into sundae dishes or one big bowl. Do this straight away as it sets very quickly.

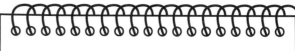

Cook's tips

You can also dissolve the jelly by placing it in a jug in the microwave with the water.

Variations

If using orange or strawberry flavoured jelly, fold in drained tinned fruit in the same flavour as the jelly after whisking the jelly and evaporated milk together. However, avoid using pineapple as it prevents the jelly from setting.

Easy option

Jelly, tinned fruit and cream.

Cook's notes

Chocolate and banana pudding

Ingredients

- 1 pint of chocolate sauce, made with:
  * 2 tbsp cornflour
  * 2 tbsp cocoa powder
  * 2 tbsp sugar
  * 1 pint of milk
  * A knob of butter
- 1 chocolate Swiss roll
- 2 bananas

Method

1. First make chocolate sauce. Blend the cornflour, cocoa powder and sugar together with enough milk to make a smooth paste.
2. Heat the remaining milk with a knob of butter until boiling, and pour on to blended cocoa mixture, stirring all the time to prevent lumps.
3. Return mixture to the pan and bring back to the boil, stirring all the time until it thickens (1–2 minutes).
4. To make up the pudding, slice the Swiss roll into six pieces and arrange in a heatproof dish.
5. Slice bananas and place on top of the Swiss roll.
6. Pour over the chocolate sauce and cover with foil. Place in pre-heated oven at 180°C or gas mark 5 for 10 minutes, until sponge has heated through.

Cook's tips

Either serve the pudding immediately from the oven, or allow to cool and serve cold.

Variations

Use a plain Swiss roll instead of chocolate, tinned fruit instead of banana, and custard instead of chocolate sauce.

Easy option

Bananas, ice cream and chocolate sauce.

Cook's notes

Strawberry meringue nests

Ingredients

- ½ pint double cream
- 4 shop-bought meringue nests
- 1 punnet fresh strawberries

Method

1. Whip the double cream and pipe or spoon into a meringue nest.
2. Wash and hull the strawberries and cut into slices.
3. Place sliced strawberries on top of the cream-filled meringue.

Cook's tips

If you want to make the sweet less fattening, you can use a mixture of half yoghurt and half double cream.

Variations

- Other fruits can be used instead of strawberries (try grapes or kiwi). Alternatively, scoop out the fruit from a passion fruit, spoon over the cream and then decorate with a couple of orange segments.
- For a grown-up sweet for a dinner party, flavour the cream with some elderflower cordial.

Easy option

Strawberries, cream and shortbread biscuits.

Cook's notes

Chocolate fruit cake

Ingredients

- 1 kg mixed dried fruit
- 160ml of chocolate milk (either ready-made in a carton, or made by mixing a chocolate powder such as Nesquik with milk)
- 2 cups self-raising flour

Method

1. Soak the fruit overnight in the chocolate milk.
2. Mix in the flour and stir until all the ingredients are thoroughly mixed.
3. Bake in an oven at 160°C or gas mark 4 for 90 minutes.
4. Test by inserting a fork or metal skewer into the centre. It should come out clean when the cake is cooked.

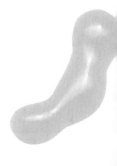

Cook's tips

- The cake serves approximately eight people—fewer if hungry!
- As dried fruit has a long shelf life, look for special offers and buy in advance (but make a note of the use-by date to ensure you use it up in time).

Variations

Top the cake with chocolate icing if desired.

Easy option

Ready-made, un-iced fairy cakes decorated with chocolate water icing and chocolate buttons.

Cook's notes

Ideas related to a Bible story or theme

Stained-glass window biscuits

Use a basic biscuit recipe, such as the one below. Roll out the dough and cut out a shape with an empty centre. Fill the centre with crushed boiled sweets and bake.

Hannah Middleton from Newcastle Upon Tyne

Ingredients

- 200g self-raising flour
- 100g caster sugar
- 100g margarine
- 1 egg, beaten
- 1 tsp lemon juice
- 150g boiled sweets in different colours

Method

1. With a rolling pin, crush the boiled sweets in a plastic bag, covered with a cloth. (This is harder than it sounds—I got my teenage son to prepare the sweets ahead of time.)
2. Rub the margarine into the flour. Stir in the sugar. Add the egg and lemon juice and mix to a stiff dough. (Dough can also be pre-prepared if desired.)
3. Knead the dough lightly and then roll out on a floured surface.
4. Cut out window shapes. Transfer to oiled greaseproof paper on a baking tray.
5. Fill the holes with crushed sweets. These will melt to make the stained glass effect.
6. Bake for 15 minutes at 180°C or gas mark 4.
7. Make sure the biscuits are cold and the 'glass' set before peeling off the paper. (NB: The set 'glass' will be very hard.)

Recipe supplied by Carole Davidson, St Luke's Church, Victoria Dock, Newham, London

Holy Communion jellies

Fill plastic disposable wine glasses with either blackcurrant or green jelly, with halved fresh grapes sunk in them. These can also be used to tell the story of the last supper.

Janet Tredrea, Cornwall Messy Churches

'Light for the world' biscuits

Use Jaffa cakes or chocolate digestive biscuits as a symbol of a dark world, with a small fondant icing star, brushed with edible glitter, stuck on. These can be used for themes about light, such as 'Jesus is the light for the world' (John 8:12) or Epiphany.

Janet Tredrea, Cornwall Messy Churches

Abraham's picnic

Spread out travel rugs randomly on the floor. Provide trays, one for each rug, holding foods that Abraham might have eaten (with a bit of a stretch of the imagination!), such as pitta bread sliced diagonally and gently warmed to be a bit crusty, hummus, paté, cream cheese, crudites, cherry tomatoes, small slices of pizza, dried apricots, dates, figs, grapes and so on.

Andover Methodist Circuit Messy Church

Star-shaped biscuits

- Make up a biscuit dough (see recipe on page 17). Add ingredients from the East, such as honey, dates, figs, apricots, pineapple, apples or sultanas.
- Roll out to a thickness of 5mm and cut into star shapes. Use a palette knife to transfer the biscuits to a baking tray lined with greaseproof paper.
- Bake in a hot oven for 10–15 minutes.
- Allow to cool and then label with flags, giving them fun and creative names such as Fig Fancy, Hot Rocks, Sarah's Surprise, Abraham's delight and so on. These biscuits could also be used for Epiphany.

Janet Tredrea, Cornwall Messy Churches

Fishy food

Make tuna sandwiches, remove the crusts and cut into fish shapes. Use to accompany the stories of Jonah; Jesus choosing his first disciples (Luke 5:1–11); the feeding of the 5000 (John 6:1–13); the fish and the coin (Matthew 17:24–27) or the breakfast on the beach (John 21:1–14).

Broomfield Messy Church, Chelmsford

Joseph's coat jelly

Layer different coloured jellies to represent Joseph's coat. Allow each layer to set before adding the next.

Joseph's coat cakes

Decorate cup cakes or gingerbread man biscuits with butter icing. Marble food colouring into the icing with a cocktail stick, and top with Smarties or jelly beans of various colours.

Jane Butcher and Lucy Moore

The wedding at Cana

Make a wedding feast of jam sandwiches, cheese spread sandwiches, iced cakes and heart-shaped biscuits. Transform your meeting area for the feast by covering tables with white disposable cloths; include a table for the 'bride and groom'. Tell the story of Jesus changing water into wine and then enjoy the feast together.

St Martin's Messy Church, Walsall

Feeding the 5000

Use ready-made plain pizza bases and decorate with various toppings to make funny faces or other designs as desired. For a sweet alternative, make individual instant trifles by placing a broken sponge finger in the bottom of a small dish, adding some tinned fruit and then topping with instant whip. Provide a selection of different sprinkles to decorate the trifles. At the end of the session, after the story, have a picnic of pizzas and trifle.

Stories about kings and treasures

Make bracelets or necklaces out of strawberry laces with 'O' shaped cereal pieces threaded on to them. Use really long laces to make necklaces and shorter ones to make bracelets.

Sandal Messy Church, Wakefield

Animal stories

Create animal faces on plain buns or round biscuits and use them to tell a variety of stories featuring animals. Cheap packs of ready-made un-iced buns or Rich Tea biscuits are best, as it is often only the topping that is eaten!

- Pigs (for stories such as the prodigal son): Spread pink icing over the bun or biscuit. Take a pink marshmallow and cut it in half to give two circular pieces, top and bottom. Use one half as the nose and cut the other piece in half again, this time across the circle, to give two semicircles to use as ears. Use two chocolate chips for the eyes. You could make white pigs to use up the other half of the packet of marshmallows—or you could just eat them!
- Birds (for stories such as the parable of the farmer): Spread yellow icing over the bun or biscuit. Use two chocolate chips as eyes. For the beak, cut a jelly diamond in half to give two triangles and stick both halves on, with the point outwards and the cut side stuck in the icing.
- Bears (for stories such as Noah's ark): Spread chocolate icing over the bun or biscuit. To make it, add some cocoa powder to icing sugar and make up to a stiff paste with water. (You could use butter cream, but water icing is cheaper and easier.) Use a chocolate button for the nose, more buttons for the ears and two chocolate chips as eyes.

Sandal Messy Church, Wakefield

Harvest fruit

- Cut apples into wedges and dip them into bowls of different coloured granulated sugar.
- Serve fruit juices in disposable shot glasses and allow people to guess what flavour of fruit they are drinking.

Janet Tredrea, Cornwall Messy Churches

Empty tomb rolls

- Using a packet of bread roll mix, make up the dough according to the recipe on the pack.
- Wrap a tennis ball sized roll around a marshmallow. Make sure the marshmallow is sealed by the dough. Bake according to the instructions on the pack.
- To test if the roll is cooked, tap it on the base. It should sound hollow.
- When you open the roll, the marshmallow will have dissolved, leaving a hollow centre to represent the empty tomb.

Jane Butcher

Palm Sunday biscuits

Make up a biscuit dough (see recipe on page 17). Roll out to a thickness of 5mm and cut into leaf shapes. Use a palette knife to transfer the biscuits to a baking tray lined with greaseproof paper. Bake at 180°C or gas mark 4 for 10–15 minutes. Allow to cool on the tray before serving.

Andover Methodist Circuit Messy Church

Cookies for everything!

Cookie cutters are available in many shapes. Make biscuits in the shapes of animals, stars, sea creatures, eggs, hearts and so on to fit in with your theme.

Messy cook's log book

Use this diary to write in the recipes you used on each date.

Date	Menu	Notes

Index

Sausage dishes

Corned beef dishes

Fish dishes

Messy desserts

Easy dessert options

Notes

Notes

Notes

Notes

Notes

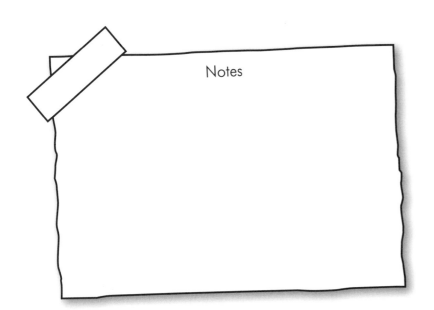

Notes

Notes

Other Messy Church® resources

Messy Crafts

A craft-based journal for Messy Church members

Lucy Moore

This book is a craft book with a difference! As well as bulging with craft ideas to inspire your creativity at Messy Church, it is also a journal to scribble in, doodle on and generally make your own.

The intention is that it will become a scrapbook of conversations, messy moments and prayers—a part of everyday life at home where you can sketch in your own ideas, list useful websites, make notes, reflect on spiritual moments, and journal your Messy Church journey.

ISBN 978 0 85746 068 4   £6.99
Available from your local Christian bookshop or direct from BRF: visit www.brfonline.org.uk.

Other Messy Church® resources

Messy Church

Fresh ideas for building a Christ-centred community

Lucy Moore

Messy Church is bursting with easy-to-do ideas to draw people of all ages together and help them to experience what it means to be part of a Christian community outside of Sunday worship.

At its heart, Messy Church aims to create the opportunity for parents, carers and children to enjoy expressing their creativity, sit down together to eat a meal, experience worship and have fun within a church context.

The book sets out the theory and practice of Messy Church and offers 15 themed programme ideas to get you started, each including:

- Bible references and background information
- Suggestions for 10 easy-to-do creative art and craft activities
- Easy-to-prepare everyday recipes
- Family-friendly worship outlines

Check out the Messy Church website at www.messychurch.org.uk.

ISBN 978 1 84101 503 3   £8.99
Available from your local Christian bookshop or direct from BRF: visit www.brfonline.org.uk.

Other Messy Church® resources

Messy Church 2

Ideas for discipling a Christ-centred community

Lucy Moore

Messy Church is growing! Since it began in 2004, many churches have picked up the idea of drawing people of all ages together and inviting them to experience fun-filled Christian community outside Sunday worship.

Following the popular Messy Church formula, *Messy Church 2* not only provides a further 15 exciting themed sessions, but also explores ways to help adults and children alike to go further and deeper with God—in other words, to grow as disciples.

As before, the material is overflowing with ideas for creativity, fun, food, fellowship and family-friendly worship, but new to *Messy Church 2* are 'take-away' ideas to help people think about their Messy Church experience between the monthly events.

Across the year, the 15 themes explore:

- Loving God, our neighbours and our world
- The life of Jesus: growing up
- Bible women: Ruth, Hannah and Esther
- Christian basics: who God is
- Baptism: belonging to the family of God
- Holy Communion: sharing and caring together

ISBN 978 1 84101 602 3   £8.99

Available from your local Christian bookshop or direct from BRF: visit www.brfonline.org.uk.

Other Messy Church® resources

Messy Church the DVD

Presented by Lucy Moore

Bringing the Messy Church story to life, the DVD is a resource to help those who are thinking of starting a Messy Church to catch the vision, and, for teams already leading a Messy Church, to help develop good practice and inspire further thinking. It features Messy Churches from a variety of situations across the UK, with parents, children, teens and leaders sharing their experiences and wisdom.

The DVD can be used to:

- introduce the concept of Messy Church.
- help a new team understand what starting a Messy Church might entail.
- help an existing team think through some of the important issues faced by leadership teams as the Messy work goes on.

For further resources to help you make best use of the DVD, visit www.messychurch.org.uk/dvd.

ISBN 978 1 84101 849 2   £9.99